This book is dedicated to friend and astrophysicist

Dr. Ryan Cooke

Special thanks to my supportive partner (and cover designer) Darcie Gray,

as well as to my superlative friends and family.

© Steven L. Smith 2018. All rights reserved.

ISBN
978-0-6483759-1-3 (ebook)
978-0-6483759-0-6 (paperback)
978-0-6483759-2-0 (hardcover)

For permission requests, write to:
steven@howtochangethe.world

www.howtochangethe.world

Part I

How to Change the World in Seven Years

Summer

History is like a cultural bank.
After many withdrawals,
today shall be my first deposit.

Though my soil is not as fertile, I will spend a lifetime attempting to grow a single rose as perfect as any in your bouquet.

I dance on your grave not to claim your ideas as my own but to keep your spirit alive.

Silence is melodic to those
who hear their own music.

The authentic individual sees unique ways of responding to the present moment that are not revealed to those who believe they have seen it all.

I feel no sorrow that I was in your
life for just the briefest of moments,
only joy that I met you at all.

By allowing me to brighten your day,
you add value to mine.

Blessed be the friend who gives you their time—the most lavish of gifts—particularly considering they do not know how much of it remains.

Words form a bridge over
the abyss that divides us.

Great people have a magnetic field stronger than any pole, a light brighter than any aurora, a gorge deeper than any canyon, but often see themselves as fridge magnets, candles and pot holes.

In our garden of memories, I plant this rose in honour of the moment we shared.

Human beings are two-dimensional;
to be happy we need only one person who
understands us and one passion that drives us.

Self-belief is speaking great truth in the face of self-doubt, which is yelling back that you have nothing left to add.

The history of your life, insofar as you have lived it, captivates my imagination more than any great war or fallen empire.

The desire for knowledge is motivated not by a love of learning, but a love of life.

Just the tip of your iceberg is heartwarming enough to warrant diving in.

The longer I spend composing each sentence to you, the deeper my bow.

What is an old friend if not the glorious unveiling of the path you did not take?

Every word spoken between two people slowly forms a memorandum of understanding, until such time when a mere glance suffices.

Autumn

All of us fall down the rabbit hole, most of us just forget how strange wonderland is.

Honesty is when a grandparent confesses that, just like Peter, they never thought they would grow old.

The problem with fatigue is not that you lack the energy to work on your projects, but rather that you must ward off the demon who whispers in your ear to cast your work into the flames.

Watching the clock is a form of passive euthanasia. Death arrives sooner than the end of a work day.

Where you see today's dimly-lit flame, I see tomorrow's bonfire. Tend to the kindling now and it will keep you forever warm.

Rekindled fire burns fiercest.

Send a letter to the friend who thinks no less of you when it takes many-a-month to thank them for the letter they sent.

The most sincere apology is to quietly become the person who no longer acts in a way that elicits an apology.

Walking slowly and without purpose is an act of rebellion in our technological age.

Only the docile find truth in questions that need no answers, only the youthful question that truth.

Knowledge is not only power but also a privilege. A black hole to the hungry is a night without a meal.

Philosophy is a heavy coat I wear.
On cold days, it keeps me warm.
On hot days, I wish I had never tried it on.

The intellectual walks a fine line between reading too much and having no original thoughts, and reading too little and having no shoulders to stand on.

This sentence has been redacted due to an unintentional copyright infringement of a statement that, in all likelihood, someone has already said.

Light refraction in the water tricks the bird into believing that the depth is shallower than it appears. Only the cormorant, who isn't afraid of getting its feathers wet, knows what wonders lie beneath the surface.

There is nothing more out of shape than a circle convincing a sphere that it should lay down flat and read, "How to be more like a circle and less like a sphere."

Only the humble moth notices the radiant bulb.

Those who cannot make peace with
their own fundamental loneliness learn
to cope by making excessive noise.

A house will never cure the symptom
of not feeling at home in the world.

This rose remains as breathtaking as the day you first picked it, but your wilted mind droops to see only its thorns.

Winter

In the silence of winter,
I heard the screams of summer.

The further we fall, the sadder we appear to those who cannot fly.

A rewording of a Friedrich Nietzsche quote, in tribute.

In times of weakness I envy that
even your sadness has its limits.

The mad were once the sad who cried away their reason.

Turbulent waves in the mind mask an endless ocean of possibilities.

When perpetrators violate their victims, it is always the latter who quietly serves the time. Ignorance is bliss to those who have committed the most heinous crimes.

The magician's dazzling smile misdirects your eyes away from their hidden scars.

After times of great suffering one must say sorry to the neglected friend, but even more so to oneself.

I am sad not because of the tears you cry,
but because you shed them for a person
who does not deserve them.

There is, and has always been, a bloody war between the masters of their own sexual impulses and the enslaved.

In the sea of repentance you will only find the victim scrubbing themselves clean.

Some people suffer from a debilitating disease that causes them to see angels as demons.

Be careful what you wish for — you may end up with a partner who loves you and children who adore you.

The extent of your pain exceeds
the limits of language.

To the clever tailors who unstitch society's patchwork blanket, take heed if you should hope to see beyond its veil, for even its greatest contributors have committed suicide.

Death paralyses those who cannot bear its silence.

From great heights I bathe in the sublime beauty of your forest, whilst you drown among the dark trees.

Spring

Purpose illuminates my darkness.

What would you do if you had only one human lifetime left to live? If carpe diem is still to mean anything at all, then it must be in the appreciation that, after billions of years, you are reading this.

It can take but a single minute to save what
would have otherwise been a day wasted,
a day to reclaim a month, a month to salvage
a year and a year to transform your life.

Joy to the risk-taker who opens the floodgates! As the water hydrates the barren plain, they discover wild flowers the likes of which never would have existed.

History teaches us that a few will achieve more in a single year than most will in a century. Only the strong break the shackles of human complacency.

When a great friend is replanted in distant soil, take solace in the fact that you were both planted in the same season.

To be a great person to the many, one should first aspire to be a great person to the few.

Loneliness is an island that can be managed by building a lighthouse. There you will see me, on my own island, shining back.

After climbing to the summit, the mountaineer is faced with that most unforgettable of truths: they are capable of reaching higher peaks still.

Reincarnation is to live so boldly that it takes the world many lifetimes to forget.

Sheep blindly follow passionate people into formidable forests, not only because their words are persuasive but also because there is an underlying admiration that, one day, they too want to become a shepherd.

Seven years is plenty of time to change the world,
but not to the person who actually will.

Part II

How to Change the World in Seven Seconds

Summer

Great art is shocking not to society
but to the artist themselves. How did
they create something so beautiful?

Destiny is forged in the minds of those who believe they are bound for greatness.

You are not alone, oh gentle gardener,
for the seeds you plant continue to flower
inside the minds of others.

Becoming an authentic person means having one foot firmly planted in the present moment, while the other soaks in the vast ocean of time.

"One day I will have an effect on this world of colossal proportions," said the patient butterfly.

To see the good in humanity is not a perspective but the physical manifestation of bringing out the best in others.

The first time we met I accepted that
I had to already let you go, for you are
a tiger and this world is your savanna.

Blessed be the lost, may they always be searching.

Grave disappointment awaits those who wish to know the secret to building a pyramid, for I know only how to place one brick at a time.

The young are eager to push the wheels of their own fate into motion, but they will not discover for some time in which direction the cart is travelling.

The human mind is like a parrot; the fact that it can talk to itself is a feat of nature, but more impressive still is teaching it to shut up.

When it feels like all the colour has been stripped from the world, like rebel fighters we must paint back with the brightest of colours.

I hear only whispers of your goodness,
though if your actions were not understated,
the world would hear your symphony.

I say to thee my fellow wanderers of the soul:
turn this world upside down to find those
rarified people whom a single moment shared
with is enough renewable inspiration to
climb a thousand mountain peaks.

Autumn

A good question illuminates
the path to many answers.

If a book falls open in a forest but
there are no humans left alive to read it,
do its words still have meaning?

At some point every freethinker will experience a turbulence of the most violent kind: a shocking realisation that their deepest held beliefs are a by-product of their immediate surroundings. If we are to ever be free of these restraints, our thinking must transcend both space and time.

To know thyself is to discover the furthermost limits of what you are capable of.

I used to worry that my best years were behind me, but time has shown the error of my thinking.

What is most harrowing about a memory is that, like a train gathering speed, the finer details begin to fade until all that remains is a blur. Nevertheless, what always remains vivid is how one felt in that moment.

To not reinvent yourself: this is a worthy regret.

Only the long-sighted can care for those in crisis,
for one must be able to see their forest from the trees.

They who claim to be an island–a paradise with no equals–soon mistake themselves for Gods.

At some point in human history, conviction became a virtue and ambiguity a vice.

The predicament with hate is that people change.

To discover a suitable balance between producing and consuming: this is my formula for a wholesome life.

Stress blocks the creative tap dry,
but keep calm and have your bottle at the ready!

In silence we learn how to decipher the noise.
In noise we learn how to appreciate the silence.

Discipline is mastering how to spend an entire day doing what others can do in a single minute.

Science fiction is alluring precisely because it takes what is closest to us (reality as we know it) and makes it peculiar. Like a fish that washes up on land, it reminds us how different life could be.

There are two fundamental questions that concern the human condition: First, why is there something rather than nothing? Second, how do we proceed with this "something" that we suddenly find ourselves amidst? There is only one book that can answer these questions and that is the one you write yourself.

As it has happened before, so it will happen again.
If you are not mindful of the time, my dear child,
then your life will be no exception.

Winter

Beware the chivalrous knight who, in insisting on rescuing the princess, becomes another dragon which she must slay.

Your beloved is not coming back. Even though you share the same bed and fall asleep beneath the same stars, they would have never thought ill of you.

The most beautiful princess in all the lands thinks herself ugly because a frog said so.

In the dead of night, I am haunted
by the ghost of your words.

I will love you until all that remains
is the memory of me loving you.

In the darkest of pits, where the air is thin and cold, one must not forget how to breathe.

The real crime was not the incident itself but the fact that, by leaving the scene, you will never know the mess you left behind.

Even the righteous path is fraught with peril.

When captaining one vessel is not enough,
you commandeer the life of another.

The theatre of the unresolved mind stages dramatic reenactments of our most evocative memories.

The key to my door does not fit your own.

Some people give away so much love that,
by the time the world sees them, they are
mistaken for someone who gives away none.

To live in the past is a type of grief:
the past is dead and it is not coming back.

Awaiting death is passive suicide for those who have grown tired of living. Hold on strong, for even if your life does not improve, the end is always near.

Underneath their helm the knight cried tears of joy.
But, because you could not see them, in your loneliest
loneliness you shot an arrow at their heart.

Only love is strong enough to pierce armour.

Twenty years from now, once you have escaped your castle, find me beneath the weeping willow. There I will tell you all of the things I wanted to tell you today.

Spring

The everydayness of being human slowly deceives us into thinking that all of this is normal. Tell me friend, do you still feel the strangeness of existence?

The phenomenon that we only experience ourselves deceives us into underappreciating not only the vast span of time that came before us, and that will inevitably come after, but also the extreme statistical improbability that our moment has arrived.

My only shortcoming, perhaps, is that I have been aiming my rocket at the moon when there is an entire universe waiting out there for me.

Inspiration in its purest form is when you inspire those who inspired you.

Have faith nomad, when you find that which you do not know you are seeking, you will have stories to tell about the time you wandered beneath ghostly skies.

Even the princess who is trapped inside
the most oppressive of towers is free
to dream up her own fairy tale.

It is the force of will, and not fate,
that pulls the stars into alignment.

Magic (of the non-supernatural kind) exists, but, like everything else in life, one must learn to become a magician. Most days you will feel like a charlatan, despondently practising in a dark gutter, but, with enough persistence, every now and then you will create a spark.

"You and I look nothing alike," said the Phoenix to its ashes.

Globetrotters yearn to fly across oceans, astronauts across galaxies. This is relativity.

This is an ode to language; the vessel in our great hunt for meaning. Here is to the past: to the cumulative power of words once said. Here is to the future: to the perfect combinations we have yet to discover.

The greatest dedication an artist
can offer their subjects is immortality.

The pioneers of yesteryear are part of the classics: stories that, despite knowing how they end, never grow old. In contrast, the lives of our contemporaries are cliffhangers; for the reader must keep themselves alive to see how the plot unfolds.

If you are carefully attuned to the sensitivities
of life, then what you will hear is not a response
but rather the voice of a kindred spirit asking
the same absurd questions as you.

I used to dream of telling my stories to the world,
but in you I found my audience.

Your claim that life amounts to nothing could not be further from the truth. The world will never be the same again precisely because you have lived.

Though a millennia has come and gone, I still hear your heart beating louder than ever. If you are reading these words a thousand years from now, do you still hear mine?

Seven seconds is plenty of time to bow, but not to the person who actually deserves it.